Text by Christina Goodings
Illustrations copyright © 2012 Amanda Gulliver
This edition copyright © 2012 Lion Hudson

The moral rights of the author and illustrator
have been asserted

A Lion Children's Book
an imprint of
Lion Hudson plc
Wilkinson House, Jordan Hill Road,
Oxford OX2 8DR, England
www.lionhudson.com
ISBN 978 0 7459 6295 5

First edition 2012
1 3 5 7 9 10 8 6 4 2 0

A catalogue record for this book is available
from the British Library

Typeset in 20/24 Baskerville MT Schoolbook
Printed in China July 2012 (manufacturer LH17)

Distributed by:
UK: Marston Book Services Ltd, PO Box 269, Abingdon, Oxon OX14 4YN
USA: Trafalgar Square Publishing, 814 N Franklin Street, Chicago, IL 60610
USA Christian Market: Kregel Publications, PO Box 2607, Grand Rapids, MI 49501

My Own Little Christmas Story

Christina Goodings
Illustrated by Amanda Gulliver

LION
CHILDREN'S

It was a spring day in Nazareth.
Mary smiled as she waved at Joseph.

"Everything is so lovely," she said.
"And soon it will be our lovely wedding day."

Later, when Mary was alone, an angel came and spoke to her.

"God has chosen you to be the mother
of his Son," said the angel. "He will bring
God's blessing from heaven to earth."

Mary was astonished, but she loved God more than anything.

"I will do as God wants," she agreed.

An angel also spoke to Joseph. He agreed
to take good care of Mary and her baby.

Soon there was more news. Only this time it was a message from the emperor. Everyone had to go to their home town to put their names on a list.

With a baby on the way, Mary and Joseph
made the long journey to Bethlehem.

The only room they could find was a stable. There Mary's baby was born. She wrapped him up snugly and laid him in a manger.

On the hillside nearby, shepherds were taking care of their sheep.

Were there wild animals nearby in the
shadows? The world could be so scary.

All at once the sky turned bright. An angel spoke:

"Good news," said the angel. "Tonight, in Bethlehem, God's Son has been born.

"He will make the whole world better."

19

Could it be true? The shepherds hurried to
the little town.

There, in the stable, they found Joseph
with Mary and little baby Jesus.

Far away, some wise men were looking at the night sky.

"Can you see that bright new star?" they exclaimed.

"It is a sign that a new king has been born."

"Let us go and find him."

Miles and miles they came. They always
trusted that the star was leading them.

It led them to Bethlehem, and the place where Jesus was. They bought out rich and royal gifts: gold and frankincense and myrrh.

Mary watched as the gift-bringers set off for their home.

"So everything is turning out as the angels told us," said Mary to herself. "And now Joseph says we must travel on, so we can keep Jesus safe.

"For when he grows up, he will bring God's blessing to everyone.

"Then they too will see heaven on earth."

29